The Mid-Life Crisis Book

By Jim Hellrood

Lisa Shilts, Editor

© 2012 by Jim Hellrood
All rights reserved.
ISBN-13: 978-1478345602

This is a work of fiction. Names, characters, businesses, places, events and incidents are either the products of the author's imagination or used in a fictitious manner. Any resemblance to actual persons, living or dead, or actual events is purely coincidental.

To my lovely wife, Lori.
I'm sorry.

Acknowledgments

God, Meghan Hellrood, Darcey Hellrood, Jeffrey Bergstrom, Brian Engebretson, Amy Brown, Baxter & Keola Exum, Brian Burrill, Jim Watson, The Amish community, Cate Walsh- Kautz, Chrisina & Jason Tofte, Dan & Sara Lange, Danielle Griffith, Deborah Richards, Denise Hubing, That guy I met that one time, Donna & Rick Pilotte, Emily Carnahan, Emily Nichols, Anakin Skywalker, Eric Dobson, Gayle Gesick, James Motor Merritt, Jamie & Chris Bates, Kyle & Jenny Kafka, The pizza dude, Jim Grisham, Joann Mancl, Sophie Schuessler, Jody Vandenburg, Joe & Laura Jandacek, Debbie Ahles, Carl & Jennie Henman, Justin & Tabitha Mooney, Karen Smith, Kelly & Jay Polk, Kimberly Smith, Laura Konrady, Laura Theravenousbraineater Herweyer, Justin Bieber, Jim & Loralei Kachel, Rob from band camp, Maria Volpe, Martin Briley, Mary Boyd, Matt Hoenecke, Mike Lotzer, Mike Mathies, Robin O'Brien, Monica Ahles, Sandi Oates, Bob & Kathy Hellrood, Sara & Scott Waltenburg, Sara Stepanik, Stormy Ward, My extremely supportive Mother, Theresa Vercimac, Gary & Terry Hellrood, Tina Grendzinski, Denver & Keryl Shilts, David & Beverly Strasser, Mary Gifford, Tricia & Kevin Smith, Vicki Frei, Zach Pagel, Brad Burrill, That chick that dumped me in high school, Jim & Kayla Griffith, Batman, Melanie Hellrood, Barry Wilson, Mark & Bonnie Gauerke, Tom Plasance, Mike Kauth, Todd & Lisa Shilts, Jeff Schuster, The Kiwanis club, Annemarie Rudolf, Luke Wolfman Ortscheid, Jim Waterman, Glen Campbell, Spencer Ahles, Jerry & Cristie Bates, Ryan Yde, Mark Ostrowski, Hallye Webb, Kristen & Kevin Wheeler, Scott Walker, Kevin Schlinkmann, Sean Duffy, Steve & Kim Brown, Matt & Ann Calcutt, Lenn E. Soderlund, That dude in the Mayhem commercials, Jill Johnson, Donna Mae, Jacki Peck, Eugene Smith, Tracy Ravey, Kevin Zinzer, Ed & Nancy Berta, Dan Landrum,...and my wife, Lori Hellrood.

Under the category of things I've learned: While interviewing for a job, it is important to resist the urge to express your feelings for the company through the art of interpretive dance.

It's a sad day when you realize that the man dancing outside your local car dealership in a chicken costume probably has a better health care plan than you do.

It's frustrating to have your identity stolen. But is it normal to have it returned with a better credit score?

I've been told that I need to work on my daily affirmations. Apparently looking in the mirror and shouting "YOU SUCK" is not a "healthy" way to start your day.

I wrestle with the same questions most men my age do:
Will I have enough in my investment portfolio to retire on?
Are my children happy and well-adjusted?
Where do I put the bodies after the crawlspace is full?

I told my wife that if something should happen to me, I'd want her to remarry. The way she said "ok" before I finished my sentence however, makes me wonder if I am completely "safe" in our home.

To all the people I've touched in my life, let me just say, I'm sorry and please don't press charges.

This week the company had a contest to see who could come up with the best "Motivational" sales phrase. Sadly, my submission was rejected: "It takes months to find a new customer - but only seconds to poke one in the eye with a stick."

It's strange how one little joke can get you labeled as having an "attitude problem", or not being a "team player". Whatever.

While in line at a fast food restaurant, the boy behind the counter asked me if I'd be requiring the "Senior" discount. In lieu of flowers, a Memorial Fund has been established on his behalf.

I'm thinking about organizing a petition drive to bring back the mullet.

I sometimes wonder if my life is actually part of a great government experiment to see whether a group of drunken monkeys could, by manipulating a series of buttons and switches, control a man's destiny. This theory would be far more palatable to me than the idea that God did it on purpose.

Under the category of "things I've learned" - When attending a sensitivity training class, it is "inappropriate" to turn to the female lecturer and say - "Hey toots, how 'bout fetching us some coffee?" Who knew?

"No boss, I think it's a great idea for me to attend weekly safety meetings for a job that I have now done for over 25 years without a recordable injury or accident.....But only if it's taught by a boy half my age, who has never done my job before."

Friends: Alienated
Family: Disowned
Job: Dead-end
Well, I think my work here is done.

Tomorrow is Justin Bieber's birthday. He was born in 1994. He feels he has "paid his dues". Somebody, please kill me now.

Stupid Mirror.

My wife has made me the man I am today. May God have mercy on her soul.

Sometimes I don't feel like I'm getting older, but then I .....Oh, wait a minute......HEY! YOU KIDS! GET OFF MY LAWN!!!........now what was I saying?

There are very few problems in life that can't be solved with a cookie and a hug. Or is that duct tape and a hammer? I forget.

My life has been one long string of awkward pauses and dramatic hesitations.

When did 50s Dress-up Day at school become 80s Retro Day? I had to explain to my daughter that I no longer own a pair of parachute pants. (Alright, I know it's not right to lie to your kids, but if she thinks I'm gonna' just hand over my MC Hammers - she's got another thing coming!)

In my life I have ridden over 100 roller coasters, camped out in a tent at -20 degrees, sang in front of over 2000 people, gone bungee jumping, and swam with sharks. At my age, not much scares me. But I just THOUGHT about spending next weekend at my mother-in-law's house.....and a little bit of pee came out.

When I was young I used to imagine I was Bo Duke. Screaming down the road in the General Lee, I'd grip the steering wheel and launch off a ramp - soaring hundreds of feet above a canyon, and landing gently like a leaf on the other side. This was my dream.
{Fast-forward 30 years} I drove my Toyota Echo through a big puddle the other day. It stalled out.

So many bad career choices. So little time.

I hope to one day be so old that I mistake the gas pedal for the brake.

If you ever get stopped by a police officer in your car, don't look at him and say, "These aren't the droids you're looking for". They hate that.

I think my mother may have been taking drugs during her pregnancy. This would account for my contempt for authority, my fear of the Amish, and the apathy I feel for the color brown.

My wife and I are like Barbie and Ken. (Providing of course Barbie is blind and has a vivid imagination.)

Does the "5 second rule" apply to pudding?

My family told me that I should be on the show, "The Biggest Loser", until they found out it was about weight loss.

I have become a walking ATM for my daughters. But instead of a PIN number, I'm voice activated. All they need to do to get money from me is - bat their eyes, look pathetic, and say those three magic words. "Daddy can I ....."

While on vacation with my family last summer, we were surprised to learn that the Rock-n-Roll Hall of Fame in Cleveland Ohio was only open until 5:30 on Fridays. This, no doubt, was a policy inspired by the famous Kiss song - "I wanna' rock-n-roll 'till 5:30, and party every day starting around 10."

Have you ever noticed how people who fail in life always have to blame someone else for why they don't succeed? Some blame their parents for not being supportive of them, some blame the government for being too oppressive, while others blame their spouses for not understanding them. In my case - I blame the Kiwanis and their stupid club! (Either them or the Amish. I haven't decided yet.)

The trick to "living the dream" is to pursue very small, easily obtainable ones. For instance, it is my dream to put a period at the end of this sentence.

There. Dream achieved!

If I were to wear a Mood Ring, it would constantly appear plaid.

While at a major crossroads in my life, one question that keeps haunting me is - am I still too young to own a Buick?

If I were Batman, I think I'd wear a flannel shirt over my costume. It's hard to be intimidating with a muffin top covering your utility belt. Seriously, have you ever tried to retrieve your Batarang while sifting through layers of fat? It ain't pretty.

The school system I attended was SO bad, there actually WAS an "I" in "team".

eat...sleep...work...eat...sleep...work...
eat...sleep...work...eat...sleep...work....
eat...sleep...work...eat...sleep...work...
long for the sweet relief that death
will bring...eat...sleep...work...
eat...sleep...work...eat...
sleep...work...eat...sleep...work...

To the girl who rejected me in High School - the one who married the astronaut, and became an oncologist on the verge of curing cancer. The one with the kids who are now a concert pianist and the youngest CEO of a Fortune 500 company, - I just made the last payment on my 2003 Toyota Echo! - SO TTHHPPPPT!!!
(ARE YA FEEL'N ME NOW???!???)

Is it just me, or does it seem as if the world has been going steadily downhill ever since Mister Rogers died?

If Hugh Hefner had to do it all over again, do you think he'd do it differently?
..............no...............of course not.........sorry, stupid question.

Does anyone know where I can get my leather pants taken out from a 28" waist to a 42"? I hear they're coming back.

All I've ever wanted was a shady place to sit, and a well-tuned guitar. ....Oh yeah - and the ability to play it.

When the Grim Reaper comes for me, he needs to know that I WON'T BE TAKEN ALIVE!!!

Ask not for whom the AARP card tolls - it tolls for thee.

I've tried "dancing like there was nobody watching", but they WERE watching - and they told me to never do it again.

Predictably, the tuna were ambivalent toward the announcement by Starkist that their product would now be "dolphin free".

Rogaine is a gateway drug to depression.

I got home today, lit a fire in the fireplace, turned up the heat, and left the door wide open as if I was born in a barn. Later, I plan to stay up real late, run with scissors, and not stop until someone gets hurt. It's great being an adult!

Our family has just put in place a new fire safety plan for our home. In the event of a fire, locate dad. He'll be the one running around in circles with his hands in the air - screaming like a little girl. After finding dad, please guide him to safety. This plan should also be followed after loud noises, Jehovah Witnesses at the door, and the occasional zombie attack.

After making a mess of my own life, maybe it's time to start living vicariously through my kids. Does anyone know where they are? I think I have 2.........or was it 3?

I've become increasingly disappointed with my status in life. By this point I had hoped to be more successful, financially secure, smarter, better-looking, and Batman.

If they ever had to amputate my legs, I think I'd like to have them reattach my feet. Then I could be the only man with wooden legs, but real feet. That would be cool.

Does anyone know where I can find a Braille copy of the Wisconsin Motorist Handbook?

Cool! I'm only 23 stomach flus away from my ideal weight.

The optimist sees the glass as half full.
The pessimist sees the glass as half empty.
I see the glass in need of Alka-Seltzer.

If I had it to do all over again - I would have bought more Beanie Babies.

Mental note: There is no place in church for trash talking. "You call that praying?? That ain't praying!! I'll show you praying!!"

Some days you're the hammer. Some days you're the nail. Some days you're just a thumb tack hanging on some useless bulletin board - wishing you had the ambition of the hammer or the usefulness of the nail, but knowing deep down inside that you're just one sore finger away from being replaced by a pretty yellow post-it note.

I'm thinking about bringing sexy back.

While walking past my daughter's collection of curling irons, straighteners, brushes, picks, and sprays, I thought I heard the hair gel mocking me.

It is my hope that one day my great-grandchildren will lead a revolt against the robot army that will no-doubt enslave us. Of course, being _my_ descendants, they will probably later complain about how much better their internet service was under the rule of their robot overlords.

While trying to rid my life of anything unproductive, I have decided to have my head surgically removed. My wife (who was surprisingly receptive to the idea), pointed out that this would not only keep my mouth from vocalizing every thought in my brain, but add a better aesthetic value to our home.

If you need proof on how bad decisions can haunt you the rest of your life - just ask my wife!

Yeesh! Get caught just once on a rooftop setting up a tripod and a high-powered rifle, and all of a sudden you're the "bad guy".

Some advice to young men: At some point you'll have to decide between pride or a wife. You can't have both. A little pride is good. It can win wars, advance a career, and make you look good in front of your friends. However, before your decision is made, remember this: Pride won't wash your underwear.

Between Life Insurance and Social Security, it would seem that I'm worth far more dead than alive. Coincidentally, my family has been encouraging me to eat more bacon, drive without a seat belt, and apply for that job on the water tower painting crew.

The other day I saw a mother leading her toddler son around on a "child leash". I remember thinking what a horrible and demeaning way to permanently damage a kid's head. After all, what are these people thinking? How will this young person ever adjust? Just what kind of emotional trauma are they inflicting? And most importantly, do they come in sizes for my teenage daughters?

I think I'm wearing my pants too high. Is it normal for a man's belt to cause chafing around the nipples?

Help! I've fallen, and I'm not really sure I want to get up!

You've heard it said that money can't buy happiness. Well trust me when I tell you that poverty ain't the way to go either!

I think I've come up with a way to defeat the Taliban through psychological warfare. Within a week I could guarantee that our enemies would be left feeling insecure, unmotivated, and questioning their very reason for existence. I'm just not sure the Geneva Conventions would allow it. Here's my plan: Step #1) Parachute my mother-in-law behind enemy lines......

"No mom. I don't think abortion is legal in the 173rd trimester."

Do you think "Star Wars" would have been Rated G if Chewbacca would have worn pants?

When my daughters were young and invited to a sleepover, I would tell them to be respectful. Always say "please" and "thank you". Now that they're older and heading to a party or concert, I just tell them not to come back too drunk or too pregnant. (Please try not to misspell my name on the Father of the Year Award.)

My doctor is trying to get me to work on my cardio. He says I have the average resting heart rate of a small woodland creature. My only question to him - is it normal to work up a sweat while eating?

When I die, I think it would be cool if there was a Flash Mob at my graveside service.

If the world were given to me on a silver platter, I'd probably take the platter and make some sort of "Death Ray" out of it. Or maybe a solar panel that could pop all our popcorn at once. People would cower in fear, shouting - "ALL HAIL THE MIGHTY POPCORN DEATH RAY!" Ok, it's decided. You keep the world, I'll take the platter.

Stupid gravity.

I forget. At what age am I supposed to start passing out pencils and pennies as "treats" for Halloween?

It's a middle-aged white guy thing, you wouldn't understand.

I don't think even Chuck Norris could use the word "Fabulous" without sounding gay.

I am constantly attempting maneuvers beyond my capability.

I think anyone who doesn't believe in world peace should be killed.

This weekend I think I'll do my impression of the grandparents from Willy Wonka and the Chocolate Factory. Only with far less charisma, enthusiasm, and dance numbers.

Do you think Ludwig Van Beethoven's work would have still been remembered if his name was Dennis Sneester?

My employer issued a new directive today. Starting tomorrow, we will be compensated not with a paycheck, but with the equivalent value of "Little Debbie Nutty Bars". At first I was bummed until I realized that I probably would have blown it on those anyway.

I think next year I'll turn over a new leaf by practicing "Random Acts of Bitterness".

90 minutes before my in-laws visit! We are at Defcon 3. Remember: no matter how you find my body, it was murder!

Been suffering the past few days with a "man cold", which as you probably know is only half as bad as a woman's cold, but we complain twice as much.

If I were the Trix Rabbit, I think I would have beaten the crap out of those kids and eaten my cereal a long time ago.

I got my hair cut this week. I asked the barber to only cut off the ones I was angry with.

I guess I shouldn't be surprised by my lack of success. In high school, I was voted "Most likely to be run over by his own truck".

Minivans are Satan's way of telling us that HE is the ruler of this world, and only HE will provide the transportation.

You know your proctologist needs to go back to med school for a refresher course when instead of using a tiny, new medical camera during a colonoscopy, he opts for the Polaroid One-Step. And if that isn't uncomfortable enough, after hearing the muffled sound of each picture being taken, he asks you to wave your butt back and forth until it's fully developed.

One of my goals in life is to one day have a disease named after me. However, with my luck, it will probably be something annoying like a rash. "Sorry, I don't think I can go swimming today, my Jim Hellrood is acting up." Maybe we could all wear Jim Hellrood Awareness ribbons.

In business, there are very few problems that can't be made worse by having more meetings.

Do they make dye for back hair? If at all possible, I'd like to leave just a little gray- 'cause it looks distinguished.

The voices in my head keep urging me to go to work and support my family. Crap! Even my psychosis has become boring.

I wouldn't say that my manager is necessarily worried about disgruntled employees, but every time I use my stapler, he dives underneath his desk and wets himself.

Sorry friend. I know you like to brag about your daughter being a professional dancer, but I don't think you can truly claim that she has a "career in the arts" if there's a pole involved.

You know you've been a parent a long time when even though nobody is around when you walk into the coffee table, you still curse like Yosemite Sam. (Rackin frackin frackin rackin rackin frackin!)

What some may regard as a complete and totally worthless exercise in futility, I call Thursday.

I told my daughter that she'd better get good grades and a scholarship 'cause Clown College ain't gonna pay for itself!

Sadly, the ratio of nose-hair trimmings to haircuts has risen to 10:1 .

You know how everything comes easy for some people? Those people suck.

My anxieties only attack when they're provoked.

Gee honey, instead of lamenting the fact that I unbutton my pants after a big meal, maybe you should be grateful I wear them at all!

The truth is, while the death of Elvis Presley at the age of 42 was tragic, it probably saved us from having to endure his '96 Comeback Special - where a badly aging "King of Rock and Roll" dressed in gold medallions and a hooded sweatshirt debuts his new rap version of "In the ghetto" to the horror of onlookers.

My father was before his time. Long before it became stylish to give our children drugs to "level out" their moods, he had a cure for A.D.D., temper tantrums, acting-up, lying, arguing, and just about all other child behavioral disorders. He called it - "A BELT".

Am I the only one who gets laughed at when at the Home Depot I tell the salesperson what broke and how I plan to fix it?

I am constantly haunted by the memory of the hair I've had cut.

If watching over 40 years of television has taught me anything, it's that sometimes shooting Gilligan is your only option.

Ladies! I know the muffin-top is impressive, but my eyes are up here! Sheesh!

My children are beginning to argue over who will take over the payments on their inheritance.

...but with every passing year, the Rascal scooter inched closer and closer to its unsuspecting prey.

Well, I brought in da noise but I seemed to have misplaced da funk.

It had been reported that 57% of the girls in our 1986 graduating class were "sexually active" in high school. I, however, was responsible for the other 43%.

I tried to get a job at the DMV, but I was told that I lack "people skills".
........yeah. That's sad.

I once thought my job was easy,
until I tried doing it sober.

It may be time for a toupee. I took my hat off the other day and a helicopter landed - thinking I was in trouble.

A medical question. If you caught Mono twice, would you then call it Stereo?

Just once, why can't it be ME who's sent to my room to think about what I've done?

Where do you go when the person you least want to be around is you?

If I'm on the "ladder of success", why does it seem like I'm always descending?

Is it "Shower praises on good-looking people who succeed" Day yet?...oh wait. That was yesterday...and the day before that...and the day before that...

Every corporate meeting I've ever been in I hear the same thing, "Think outside the box", "There is no 'I' in team", "Don't put that in your mouth, you don't know where it's been", etc. . . . . .

In a world filled with back-handed compliments and intellectual insults - for my money nothing works better than a good old fashion mooning!......Which is probably why my career in politics never took off.

At first I was concerned when my daughter's date came to pick her up wearing a court-ordered GPS tracking anklet. But then I figured - "Well, at least I know she'll make curfew."

Maybe I'm just paranoid, but I think I just saw the devil on my left shoulder fist-bump the angel on my right.

Although I only have 218 friends on Facebook, I am comforted by the fact that I have no enemies.

Seriously, is it too much to ask for the Texas Roadhouse to have a licensed cardiologist on staff????

Playing Whack-A-Mole is always fun….unless of course, you're the mole.

If I were stranded on a deserted island and given three wishes by a genie, I'm not entirely sure one of them would be to be rescued.

It's like I always say, "If at first you don't succeed, quit. And whine about it in a book!"

Printed in Great Britain
by Amazon